Discovering
OIL LAMPS

Cecil A. Meadows

Shire Publications Ltd.

CONTENTS

ACKNOWLEDGEMENTS

The author would like to acknowledge the valuable help he has received from the trade catalogues of Sherwoods Ltd. of Birmingham, the former Lighting Trades Ltd. of London S.W.18, and Falk Stadelmann Ltd. of Farringdon Road, London E.C.1.

Without the list of Falks much of this book would not have been possible for they were the foremost firm engaged in the distribution of oil lamps and accessories.

1. PRIMITIVE AND EARLY LAMPS

The first lamps were made from stone by Palaeolithic man. The requirements were simple: a stone with a small depression in the top and of suitable shape to be held in the hand and to stand level. The reservoir at the top to hold the fuel of animal fat was carefully hollowed out and a small sloping groove was cut to take the wick of bark or fibre. Where soft stone such as sandstone was available the manufacture of lamps was easy, but the early lamps of south India were made of granite and could be fixed to walls as well as being made to stand.

In his *Life in Ancient Britain* N. Ault suggests that stone lamps dated from the Magdalenian Period (15,000 BC) and Dr Karl Absalon has dated a Moravian lamp at 30,000 years old. Stone lamps have been found in Cyprus dating from about 4,000 BC and many finely decorated ones from Crete, some even on pedestals, have been placed at 1,500 BC.

Many Romano-British lamps were of chalk, oval, square or round, whilst in Alaska the Eskimo lamps were finely carved from hard stone, circular or sad-iron shaped, with moss as a wick and blubber for fuel. Eskimo lamps are known carved from igneous rock as large as 16 inches long and 6 inches deep.

Shell lamps

The next development was the use of shells—easily obtainable in most places and practically ready for use. Certainly shells were used for lamps in Ur, Mesopotamia, and the Mediterranean area.

In Orkney and Shetland suspended lamps called buckies were made from the shell of the red whelk, while the Welsh used oyster shells with rag wicks. Scallop, whelk and oyster shells were widely used in Europe with fish oil as the common fuel.

Gradually lamps of other materials came to be made in shell form. In the Near and Middle East alabaster was used and scallop-shaped pottery lamps have come from Malta, Cyprus, Crete, Sardinia and Phoenicia.

During the Canaanite period in Palestine lamps in shell form were made of bronze and the iron crusie type of lamp of northern Europe (see page 5) is a development from the shell style.

The open bowl or saucer type of lamp was a manufactured development of the hollowed stone of earlier centuries. Herodotus (c.485-425 BC) refers to the Festival of Lamps in which lamps in the form of flat saucers were used. These were filled with a mixture of castor oil and salt, upon which the wick floated.

The ancient Chinese lamp consisted of an open saucer, sometimes mounted on feet, with a floating wick. Bronze and limestone were favourite materials and use was frequently made of a central spike as a wick support. Korean, Chinese and Japanese lamps in the Smithsonian collection are made of porcelain, pottery, brass, iron and pewter and are mainly of the saucer type, some adapted for hanging.

Throughout the Pacific light was provided by coconuts with floating wicks and the open saucer *lamparistas* of Brazil used peanut oil for fuel. Nigerian lamps were simple lipped bowls, sometimes with the wicks protruding through a spout, whereas the majority of Indian lamps had wide spouts which enabled thicker wicks to be used, giving a greater light.

Greek and Roman lamps

Excavations of fourth- and fifth-century mosaics reveal details of conical and vase-shaped float-wick suspension lamps, many of them made of glass and in the East richly ornamented for use in palaces and mosques. This type of lamp remained unchanged until well into the Middle Ages and stand models are known which resembled a large goblet with a float wick which rested in a metal support fitted to the rim or to a central spike.

Egyptian lamps were mainly of the open-footed type with a bowl, an open spout or long lip, and a carrying handle at the back somewhat like an open feeding cup. Greek lamps owed much to the earlier Egyptian style but showed many improvements. The Greeks curved the hitherto straight rim, possibly to reduce splashing when filling, and covered the open nozzle or lip and made it into a spout. Using the potter's wheel they mass-produced lamps, mainly black, designed to burn olive oil. Bronze lamps were made, but these were not common.

Roman lamps closely resembled the Greek, though in many cases the bowl was more depressed. The wick was of vegetable fibre (verbascum or papyrus) and tweezers were used for trimming. The lamps were both glazed and unglazed and in an infinite variety of style and nozzle formation. Many lamps were in bird or animal form and were decorated with figures of deities.

Parthian lamps were very similar, being wheel-made and generally having long nozzles, which often pointed downwards, though the downward nozzle does not appear to have had any special advantage. Sesame oil made from the plant *Sesamum*

PRIMITIVE AND EARLY LAMPS

STONE

ROMAN

ARAB

17TH CENTURY
ENGLISH
COPPER

CRUSIE

OPEN
STAND

indicum was generally used.

Frequently Roman and Greek lamps were multi-spouted and either hung from the ceiling by means of chains or stood on a stand or *candelabrum*. The word *candelabrum*, originally a candlestick, was later used to describe a stand for lamps, and these were made of wood or bronze and consisted of a plinth, shaft or stem and a foot. They were often adjustable and in the better examples the stem was in the form of a figure. These figures supported the lamps on chains and had a small trimming needle. The lamps (*lucernae*) burned perfumed oil.

A lamp found at Pompeii had as many as fourteen lights and a shop in Herculaneum had a huge multi-spouted bronze lamp suspended from the centre of the ceiling. In later times many Roman lamps had Christian symbols on them and were known to have been made of both iron and pewter.

Hebrew and Indian lamps

The early seven-branched candlesticks of the Hebrews frequently grouped float-wick lamps of the open saucer type, burning olive oil. The *hanukkah* or *chanukkah* of Leviticus was a row of eight spoon-shaped lamps or spouted saucers, sometimes incorporating a pilot lighting device.

Indian temple lamps closely resembled the Hebrew. They were mainly of the open saucer type but with the traditional cobra handle and often supported by a female figure. Many of the vase types with a reservoir were equipped with a spoon so that worshippers could purchase oil by the spoonful. Most of these were just to give a votive light rather than to provide illumination. The lamps could be of the hanging or pedestal type, often in the shape of a stylised swan, and were multi-spouted.

In Ceylon gravity-fed lamps were used, rather like a bird fountain, where the oil was supplied to the wick in a tube by the pressure of gravity. Where these were of the hanging type they resembled a bird whose body was the reservoir with a trough at its feet. They were made of brass and examples have also been found with the lamp made in the shape of a lotus flower.

In the fifth century BC bronze lamps in Palestine were similar to their Greek contemporaries and Etruscan lamps of the same period are known in bronze, with as many as sixteen nozzles, and richly ornamented with sirens, satyrs, and animals.

Medieval lamps

Lamps in medieval times had remained unchanged for centuries, there having been no advance since Roman times. The documents of the period rarely mention lamps and very few illustrations appear in paintings or sculptures. Many medieval British lamps were made of iron and so few have survived. Early lamps made in England were of crude earthenware, spoutless and with a floating wick, a type unchanged for a thousand years in Europe. Viking ships had open saucer lamps with a spike for sticking into a convenient crevice. Lamps of brass of the open pan type with tiered reservoirs and taps for the drawing of oil were known in Antwerp. The sixteenth-century lamps of Norway were large iron pans with spouts at four corners and smoke shields and were used with cod-liver oil. Cresset stones with multiple depressions have been found in many northern parts and provided the simplest form of primitive light.

Crusie lamps

Crusie lamps of Celtic origin date from the early Iron Age and were generally double-bowled, frequently with a toothed rack arrangement. The lamp still had a single wick; the second bowl merely acted as a drip catcher and provided a safety factor. They were widely used in Orkney, Shetland, the Hebrides, Scotland and Ireland with fish oil as fuel. A similar type was used in the Channel Islands under the name of *croiset* or *crasset*. Superstitions concerning them told that a blue flame meant wind next day, a green flame meant witches and a spark meant news to the person in whose direction it flew.

The Cornish variety was called a *chill* and, apart from earthenware lamps, the Cornish used mussel shells. In the Scilly Isles the crusie type was sometimes lidded while the open type occurred in square shape with a spout at each corner. The type was widely used in the Low Countries, France and remote lands like Iceland and some of these specimens were known to have been made of brass.

Similar lamps in the United States were called 'Phoebe lamps' or, when fitted with a support or channel, 'Betty lamps', probably introduced by the German colonists in Pennsylvania.

Animal lamps

The animal kingdom has provided man with light in many parts of the world. In Orkney and Shetland the bodies of stormy petrels, with wicks inserted in their throats, were used as lamps. In Venezuela the nestlings of a nocturnal bird, the guacharo, were boiled down for oil and fat for light, while in Japan sea-urchins were filled with fish oil and fitted with wicks. In many primitive areas sheep skulls were used as lamps and in British Columbia the oily candle-fish was used for lighting, with a strip of bark inserted as a wick.

Spout lamps

Spout lamps, which resemble a globular teapot with the spout upturned and fitted with a drip collar, were made of brass, pottery, iron, pewter or tin, according to their country of origin and persisted in use from Roman times to the nineteenth century. The main fuel was whale oil, changing later to colza (vegetable oil), but in the Mediterranean olive oil was widely used. These spout lamps often had a stand and were frequently fitted with a strap at the back for hanging on a hook. Many were double-spouted with a hinged or removable cover. The *lucernae* of Italy, Spain, Portugal and Greece could be raised or lowered on a central stem and had three or four spouts. They were fitted with trimmers, prickers for raising the wicks, and tweezers and were the most advanced form of spout lamp. The Dutch and Flemish versions resembled coffee pots and were often elaborately decorated. The spout lamp was definitely of European origin, and the American lamps were based on originals from Germany and Holland.

Colza lamps

Colza lamps provided the great link between the primitive form of teapot- and saucer-shaped lamps and the highly efficient paraffin lamps of the mid nineteenth century. They represented the application of mechanical ingenuity to the provision of better domestic lighting, for the oil lamp as an efficient means of lighting really dates from the end of the eighteenth century. Leger of Paris invented a flat-wick lamp in 1783 which laid the foundation stone, for the wick was soon changed to a circular form.

In 1784 Amie Argand, a Geneva physicist, invented a round burner with a tubular wick and an iron chimney. His partner, Quinquet, made a significant improvement by producing a glass chimney instead of the clumsy iron one. These lamps used vegetable oil (colza) as fuel and their efficiency was greatly improved by Carcel's invention in 1800 of a clockwork pump for raising and feeding the fuel.

The Carcel lamp remained the principal oil lighting device until 1836 when Franchot produced his famous Moderator lamp. The Moderator had a spring-loaded piston to give pressure to the feed and was not replaced until after the invention of the refining process for paraffin in 1847 and the subsequent development of lamps to suit the new fuel. In America a clockwork lamp on the general lines of the Carcel was invented by Diacon in 1840, closely followed by the Solar lamp of the same year.

By its nature colza oil was somewhat sticky, and unless the lamps were cleaned frequently the burners tended to 'gum up'. Thus when colza lamps and paraffin lamps were available side by side, as they were in the 1860s and early 1870s, the paraffin lamp won the day because of its simplicity and the cheapness of its fuel.

2. RUSHLIGHTS AND CANDLES

A parallel development to domestic oil lighting from Roman times until well into the last century was the use of rushlights and candles. The Romans are reputed to have invented the candle in the years soon after the birth of Christ, and both tallow (animal fat) and beeswax were used. Some three centuries later the Phoenicians were using candles of bleached wax.

In the monasteries large apiaries were kept so that beeswax could be used for candle making. Candles made from beeswax were superior to those of tallow and required little attention when burning. At the Norman Conquest the English were using splinters of wood dipped in wax and the candle did not come into general use in this country until the fourteenth and fifteenth centuries. At this time the guilds of wax and tallow chandlers developed the industry and exercised control over quality.

Candles were first made by dipping, layer after layer, until the invention of the candle mould in the fifteenth century, followed in the nineteenth century by the candle-making machine. In the eighteenth century spermaceti from the whale provided a new material for high-grade candles and in the mid nineteenth century paraffin-wax candles were cheap, plentiful —and not edible! For even the Eddystone Lighthouse was first lit by candles and the Elder Brethren of Trinity House were concerned about the way that the lighthouse-keepers used to eat the tallow candles to help out their rations.

Links and flambeaux, which were used by runners to light the way for carriages and sedan chairs, were made from rope dipped in fat or resin. Rushlights, which were widely used, and quite economical, were made from partly peeled rushes dipped in tallow. One 2-foot rushlight would burn for about an hour and this meagre light was the sole illumination in the homes of the poor for centuries.

In the present day the candle is still used for emergency lighting, and in the form of night lights for children's bedrooms. It is also still widely used for devotional purposes and for altar lighting in Christian churches throughout the world.

3. PARAFFIN LAMPS

History of mineral oil

Oil has been known and used since biblical times but only since the discovery of refining processes has its use become widespread. Simply, the refining or distillation processes produce petrol, paraffin (kerosene), diesel and light fuel oils, heavy oils and bitumens. Thus paraffin is a mixture of liquid hydrocarbons obtained by the distillation of petroleum (mineral oil) or of coal and bituminous shale. Before the days of the motorcar the petrol content of the crude petroleum was thrown away as being of no value and in fact dangerous. Though Reichenback and Christison discovered paraffin simultaneously in 1830, it was not until James Young, a Scot, discovered a refining process in 1847, patented in 1850, that real strides were made. Young successfully used his discovery as an illuminant at Riddings coal mine at Alfreton in Derbyshire. His process of distillation was first applied to shale from the Scottish Lowlands, and he founded a company, later absorbed by the British Petroleum Company, known as Young's Paraffin Oil Company. He can thus be called the father of the oil industry for he was ten years ahead of the oil drilling in the U.S.A., though his was oil from shale and not natural petroleum.

The discovery of natural oil

The word *petroleum* means 'rock oil' and shale is oil-bearing rock made millions of years ago from mud and silt, decaying vegetable matter and microscopic marine life. For more than two centuries oil had been known to exist in Pennsylvania in natural springs, and much was sold as Seneca oil, a medicine. It was known as a burning fuel but in its crude state was far too smoky as a domestic illuminant.

George H. Bissell, an American lawyer, saw the possibilities of large-scale oil production and with other interested parties sent a man out to test for oil on a commercial scale. This man, Edwin L. Drake, a handyman with an ability for hard work, commenced his search in May 1858. On 27th August 1859 his efforts were rewarded when the well that he had drilled, some $69\frac{1}{2}$ feet deep, filled with oil.

In the first 24 hours his well pumped 25 barrels, the news of which caused a rush of prospectors. Land in the Oil Creek area was quickly sold or leased and by the end of 1860 over half a million barrels had been produced from some 70 wells. In early 1861 at the mouth of Oil Creek a gusher, which flowed at the rate of 3,000 barrels a day, was struck and the huge quantities of gas resulted in a serious explosion which caused the deaths of nineteen men. By the end of 1864 there were over 500 oil companies and the industry was beginning to plan for improved techniques and equipment.

Three years after Drake had struck oil a young man of 23 called John D. Rockefeller formed a company in Cleveland, Ohio, to refine oil scientifically and in five years he became a dominant figure in the refining industry. He realised that control of the wells was essential and in 1870 he founded the Standard Oil Company and arranged with the railways for special low freight charges. Thus in a few years he was able to gain control of nine tenths of the refineries and by streamlining methods of distribution the American kerosene industry was put on a sound and efficient basis.

Royal Dutch Shell

It was not until the late 1880s that the Dutch oil industry in Sumatra began and the volume of production was not internationally significant until the beginning of the present century. J. B. August Kessler founded the Royal Dutch Company at The Hague in 1890 and began acquiring small units and welding them into one organisation. The potential of the Chinese market fascinated him and he engaged a young man named Henri Deterding to open up that market. They had the advantage over Standard Oil in that they were much nearer, but the transport facilities were lacking. A deal was made with Marcus Samuel, head of Shell, and so the mighty Royal Dutch Shell group was formed. Marcus Samuel and Company at first were distributors for Russian kerosene supplied by Rothschilds and when they acquired a concession in Borneo they turned their efforts to Far Eastern oil and the problem of its transportation.

In 1892 Marcus Samuel launched the first steam tanker to go through the Suez Canal, the *Murex*, forerunner of the huge Shell fleet whose ships are still named after shells. The name 'Shell' derives from Marcus Samuel's original business as an importer of souvenir boxes covered with sea shells and a dealer in mother-of-pearl.

In 1901 Weetman Pearson, later Viscount Cowdray, the head of a large firm of engineering contractors, coming back from Mexico missed his connection at Laredo, Texas. There, much local excitement about oil discoveries made him think of the oil seepages he had seen in Mexico. Pearson determined to get options on the land surrounding the seepages and in a few years he spent some £5 million on the project. The famous Potrero No. 4, struck in 1910, flowed at the rate of 100,000 barrels a day for sixty days and when under control ran for 8 years and produced 100 million barrels. In 1919 Royal Dutch Shell took over the Mexican Eagle company formed by Pearson and thus gained a foothold on the American continent.

The Anglo-Persian Oil Company

Though ancient Persian records mentioned surface deposits of petroleum, it was not until 1901 that W. K. D'Arcy made an agreement with the Persian government giving him the right to explore for oil in the south-west. They worked for seven years with little success but at the last moment when funds were exhausted they struck oil in enormous quantities. The Anglo-Persian Oil Company was formed and a refinery was built at Abadan at the head of the Persian Gulf. By 1913

Persian crude oil was being refined at Abadan and shipped away to world markets. In May 1914 the British government entered into an agreement with the Anglo-Persian Oil Company and invested some £2 million to acquire 51 per cent of the ordinary shares. Today the Middle Eastern oil-fields supply a large part of the world's oil.

Developments in lamp design

The discovery by James Young in 1847 of his refining process which produced paraffin marked the start of the era of oil as the universal illuminant. Thus the oil-lamp age and the Victorian age were synonymous.

The introduction of the flat wick using paraffin, with its spurred wheel or cog adjustment, and a design which produced good aeration of the flame laid the foundation of the great Victorian lamp industry.

In 1865 Joseph Hinks placed two flat wicks side by side and invented the Duplex burner which was both reliable and efficient. The effect of the two lighted wicks in close proximity increased the luminosity of the flame. This burner, fitted with an extinguishing device, took an oval bulge chimney which had to be fitted with the wicks parallel to the length of the bulge. This burner, virtually unchanged, is still made today and is widely used in greenhouse heaters as well as lamps.

Between the years 1859 and 1870 some eighty patents a year were applied for concerning oil lamps, the research being aimed at producing better light. Draught design of both the burner and chimney together as a unit was the key factor.

With the coming of the central draught burner, that is a lamp with a tubular wick and a hollow draught tube in the centre, a more efficient flame was produced with capacities up to 200 candlepower.

The central draught lamps had spreaders or air diffusers of many different types fitted into the central tube and it is important to note that the burner will not function if the spreader is missing and will smoke if the spreader is distorted or broken.

The chimney plays an essential part in producing a flame of maximum luminosity and, where chimneyless lamps such as the Wanzer or Kranzow were used, a clockwork-operated fan was necessary to give sufficient air to prevent smoking and to provide a suitable flame.

In between the flat-wick burners and the central-draught type were those called Kosmos which took a flat wick but which came out circular in the burner. The draught was still taken from the sides of the burner as in the flat-wick type and the burner had no spreader like the central-draught type. The Kosmos burner was confined in use to small hand lamps and reading lamps.

Household usage

Even the most modest households of Victorian times had several lamps for different purposes, for virtually each room had to have its own lamp. The parlour or front room would certainly have a Duplex lamp with a globe or perhaps a 50 candlepower central-draught lamp. The dining-room would have a Duplex lamp in a cheaper version, while in the kitchen the table lamp would have a 1-inch burner with no globe or perhaps a small hanging or harp lamp. For bedroom lighting small hand lamps were the normal thing. They were made in a wide range of sizes and qualities to suit the light required and the pocket of the purchaser. Night lights for the children and a small wall lamp for the lavatory brought the total number of lamps employed in a small dwelling to about a dozen. These lamps all had to be cleaned frequently, wicks trimmed, founts filled with oil and glasses and globes washed and polished. They represented quite an item in the long list of household chores.

In larger and wealthier households there might be some 36 lamps or more and frequently one of the servants did little else but clean and maintain them. Many were made of brass, the polishing of which added considerably to the labour. Special tools were available for lamp maintenance such as wick trimmers and wash leather pads on wire handles for chimney cleaning. To protect ceilings glass or enamel shades or smoke bells were suspended over the lamps and chimneys were fitted with small mica tops to restrict the rising heat and smoke.

Lamp decoration

Naturally the design of oil lamps followed the current trends in fashion in an age of great variety in design and embellishment. The cheaper opal glass founts of table lamps were generally decorated with floral motifs and their cast iron stands with leafy, floral or Gothic patterns. Many of the daintier small lamps of white opal glass had small roses and rosebuds painted all over them. The medium-priced table lamps with their polished black ceramic bases and brass pillars often had fluted tanks of ruby, amber, green or blue glass reflecting the robustness of the Victorian age. The better-quality table lamps had cut-glass founts and were frequently mounted on Corinthian pillars, the finish of which included silver plate as well as antique copper, satin or polished brass.

A range of small reading and table lamps made from spelter, finished in antique copper and fitted with Kosmos burners, were quite popular. These lamps had relief designs of cherubs, cupids or other classical motifs; in some cases strong Gothic patterns were used. With cast iron brackets for wall lamps and suspensions for hanging lamps, the material lent itself to generous decoration. Elaborate floral or geometric designs, incorporating the figures of animals and birds, were commonplace; even the links of the hanging chains were ornamented.

The spherical and tulip-shaped glass globes had etched or sandblasted designs, mainly of flowers and leaves with geometrical and classical motifs.

Chimneyless paraffin lamps

Among the interesting Victorian inventions in the realm of oil lighting were the series of chimneyless lamps. With an ever-widening export market, particularly to frontier posts and primitive areas, the fragility of glass chimneys and globes posed a problem.

The answer was found in a clockwork-driven fan to assist the natural draught and to provide a clear flame without a chimney. The earliest specimens were the Wanzer, the Britannic, and the Hitchcock, which was the first in the field in 1868.

In Falks' catalogue of 1912 a new Hitchcock lamp was advertised as follows: 'This lamp is an improvement on the old pattern. It burns longer and it gives about 75 per cent more light because the flywheel is now placed vertically which prevents dust from lodging on its wings and the working parts are reduced to 44, about one half less than in the old lamp. . . . The old pattern winds from underneath, the new type winds horizontally in side of the base.'

Another chimneyless lamp, made by Sherwoods of Birmingham, was the Kranzow, vast quantities of which were exported all over the world. Production was maintained until a few years ago.

Though efficient, chimneyless lamps were not widely used in homes, partly because of cost, but also because of the risk of fire from the unprotected flame.

Incandescent lamps

The incandescent mantle was developed by Von Welsbach after many experiments between 1885 and 1893, following those of Clamond in 1881.

The mantles were made of silk or cotton fabric impregnated with a mixture containing thorium with a trace of cerium.

These mantles, when suspended in the flame of an oil or gas lamp, produced a high luminosity, thus providing the basis for the incandescent lamp.

Paraffin-burning incandescent mantle lamps may be divided into two classes, pressure and non-pressure. The non-pressure variety consists of those lamps, such as Famos and Aladdin, designed specifically as incandescent lamps, and the conversion type, such as Kronos or Candesco, which were mantle burners with a Duplex fitting. This type enabled owners of Duplex flat-wick table lamps to convert them, by exchange of burner, to an incandescent light rated at 80 to 100 candlepower. These lamps had an upright mantle with a straight or slightly bulged chimney of $2\frac{1}{8}$-inch fitting.

A small mantle lamp of French manufacture, the Titus, was popular for some years and used methylated spirit as a fuel. This is a clean and pleasant fuel but in Britain, owing to its cost, it never became universal.

The Famos and Aladdin non-pressure lamps remained for many years and the latter is still in production. The Aladdin burner has been improved in minor ways but remains basically the same, though now with a locking device for both chimney and mantle.

Pressure lamps

There were many types of pressure lamps and lanterns, though the principle was basic: the pre-heating with methylated spirits of a generator tube.

When the fuel tank was pumped full of air the fuel was forced through the heated generator and vaporised, igniting as it left the tiny hole in the nipple or end of the generator. Simple to use, the main requirements are that the generator must be heated adequately and that sufficient pressure must be maintained in the tank, which gives a most economical result owing to the high proportion of air consumed.

Pressure lamps and lanterns were made by firms experienced in the making of pressure stoves for they used the same principle as a Primus stove. It was possible to buy an adaptor unit which would stand on the top of a Primus stove and convert it to a mantle pressure lamp. The Swedish Primus, the American Coleman and the British Veritas, Tilley and Vapalux (Aladdin) accounted for a large part of the market in pressure lighting and though the domestic demand waned the portable lantern is still sold in quantity to industry and to the developing nations. The portable floodlights are still widely used in civil engineering projects and for emergency air strips, though many of them now use propane gas instead of paraffin.

Many Coleman lamps from North America were available with petrol as a fuel, but they were never widely used in Britain, possibly because paraffin was naturally considered a safer fuel for home use.

Glassware

The main source of lamp chimneys was Saxony—many of them were marked 'Best Saxony Crystal'—while the majority of the incandescent chimneys came from Jena. Much lighting glassware came from France and Belgium and when German supplies ceased in the First World War quantities were made in Britain, though of an inferior quality.

By the time of the Second World War the oil lamp had largely disappeared, but with the interruption of electricity supplies by bombing they were once more in demand. Again home-produced glassware had to fill the bill, though fair stocks existed in the ironmongers' warehouses.

The uninitiated might think that any chimney which fits a burner would do, but this is not so; the most critical factor of an oil lamp is the draught supply, which is calculated very accurately. The chimney, by the size and location of the bulge and the overall height, is the ruling factor and substitutes will not give the same lighting efficiency.

The use of the word 'globe' does not of necessity mean that it is of spherical shape. The globe was the additional glass for the diffusion of light, whereas the chimney was essential to the burning of the lamp. Many ornamental chimneys were made which were used without globes but the majority of table lamps used a globe of some shape or other.

Most shades and globes were imported, though in later years parchment shades became common and synthetic materials were used for the shades of incandescent lamps.

Though the Victorians mainly had glass shades many of their standard lamps had elaborate creations of silk ornamented with beads and tassels, though for safety a clear interior glass globe was often used as well.

Where the lamps were designed or modified for heating purposes chimneys and globes of ruby glass were used and the general effect was a comforting glow.

4. INDUSTRIAL AND MARINE OIL LIGHTING

The widespread use of neon strip lighting and fluorescent tubes for industrial and commercial use is so much a part of the everyday scene that it is difficult to imagine an age when oil and gas between them had to do duty instead.

Street lighting in rural Britain, where it existed at all, was by means of oil lamp, generally the same type of standard as gas, but with founts of the 50 or 100 candlepower type of central draught, similar to the Veritas. Similarly yard lanterns or those designed for wharves, verandahs or stables were available, usually with Duplex burners, singly or in pairs. Even today there are remote railway stations with oil-lit platform lamps of this type, sometimes with the Duplex fount replaced by a pressure lamp of the Tilley type.

Catalogues of the last half of the nineteenth century and the first few years of the twentieth show portable lanterns on tripods described as suitable for street lecturers, an interesting reminder of the immense changes today in the dissemination of knowledge.

Railway lighting involved not only the stations and yards, but the engines, rolling stock, signals, signal-boxes and crossings as well. All of these were made for their specific purposes and in many cases remained unaltered for a century or more. The torch type of lamp, still used in some cases out of doors in emergency work to rail track or in industrial projects, has remained virtually unaltered and its design can be clearly traced back to the spout lamps of Roman times.

Following the crude inverted flare lamps with naphtha as fuel and used mainly by barrow boys came the inverted pressure lamps from 200 to 1,000 candlepower. These were widely used for market stalls and travelling fairs and provided a high standard of illumination. Catalogues of the period advertise these lamps, of which the Blanchard was a well-known type, as being suitable for shop fronts, railway stations, galas, camps and fairs. The travelling showmen and circus proprietors of Victorian times had an amazing variety of these lamps, always highly polished and in impeccable condition, for their very livelihood depended on light—portable, quick, reliable and available in all weather conditions.

Lighthouses

From earliest times religious houses near the coast displayed lights for the guidance of mariners and in medieval times they were certainly provided by oil lamps. Naturally candles played a large part in early marine warning lights and though oil displaced candles at North Foreland in 1787, coal lighting died hard. It was not until 1816 that coal gave way to oil on the Isle of Man; the last coal light at St. Bees, Cumberland, was in 1822, while Dungeness did not change to oil until 1831.

The first use of flat-wick oil lamps for lighthouse illumination was at Liverpool in 1736 but it was not until Argand invented his circular-wick burner in 1784 that effective illumination was possible. The early fuels were vegetable oils such as olive and coconut but colza eventually became established because of its lower cost. Sperm oil was also used but by 1846 colza was only a third of the cost of sperm, and the latter became obsolete. The production of mineral oils soon eliminated its rivals and by 1873 reliable light mineral oils were available.

The Bude lamp followed the Argand and it had intense combustion due to the introduction of oxygen into the centre of the wick. Some lamps of this type in France are recorded as having lasted unattended for as long as three months. The development of this vapour burner was accelerated and by 1921 the pressure burner and incandescent mantle as used today were being fitted almost everywhere.

Though electricity has for many years replaced oil in navigation lamps, the latter fuel is still used for emergencies, and stand-by oil navigation lights are standard practice.

Vehicle lamps

The majority of vehicle lamps were fitted with colza burners because of the brighter light and ability to keep alight in windy conditions. Conversion of carriage lamps from candles to oil was made possible by replica metal candles fitted with a wick burning paraffin. Traction engines and omnibuses and similar large vehicles used sturdy flat-wick colza burners with wicks up to 1 inch and omnibuses generally had a lamp with a large semi-circular glass front.

Motor-cars, making their appearance at the end of the nineteenth century and needing good illumination, had large brass lamps with plated reflectors and lenses. Later acetylene provided a more powerful light, leaving the oil lamps for the side and tail, and these in turn gave way to electricity.

¾ TABLE LAMPS

TABLE LAMPS WITH ¾″ BURNER WERE USUALLY OF THE CHEAPER VARIETY. THE BURNER, RATHER A SMALL ONE FOR TABLE LAMP USE, WAS USED MAINLY FOR HAND LAMPS.
THE BULGE CHIMNEY WAS MADE IN TWO HEIGHTS, SHORT FOR HAND LAMPS AND TALL FOR TABLE USE, 1¾″ FITTING

CAST FOOT, DECORATED GLASS FOUNT FITTED WITH ¾″ BURNER

JAPANNED BODY, ¾″ BURNER, SANDBLAST GLOBE

BRASS BODY, BLACK CHINA BASE, ¾″ BURNER, SANDBLAST GLOBE

COMMON JAPANNED BODY, ¾″ BURNER, NO SHADE. THE CHEAPEST TYPE OF TABLE LAMP

BRASS PILLAR FOUNT, ¾″ BURNER AND OPAL VESTA SHADE

1″ TABLE LAMPS

1″ SLIP BURNER, COMMON
TINPLATE BODY,
JAPANNED IN COLOURS

1″ SLIP BURNER, COLOURED
GLASS OPTIC FOUNT AND
CAST IRON BASE

1″ SLIP BURNER,
POLISHED BRASS BODY

1″ SLIP BURNER, DECORATED
GLASS FOUNT AND
CAST IRON BASE

1″ SLIP TABLE LAMPS WERE EXTREMELY POPULAR AND
LOW PRICED, THE EVERY DAY TABLE LAMP FOR THE
COTTAGE. THE No. 10 BULGE CHIMNEY HAD A $2\frac{1}{16}$″
FITTING AND THOUGH SHADES COULD BE FITTED THESE
LAMPS WERE USED MAINLY WITH CHIMNEY ONLY

DUPLEX LAMPS

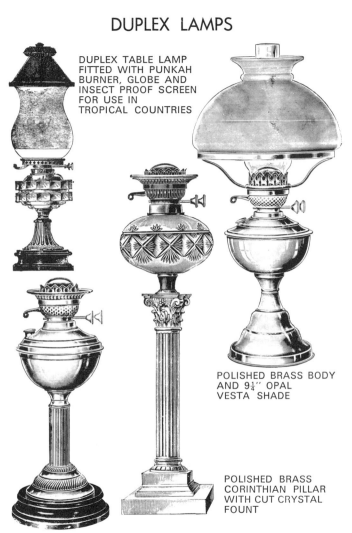

DUPLEX TABLE LAMP FITTED WITH PUNKAH BURNER, GLOBE AND INSECT PROOF SCREEN FOR USE IN TROPICAL COUNTRIES

POLISHED BRASS BODY AND 9¼" OPAL VESTA SHADE

POLISHED BRASS CORINTHIAN PILLAR WITH CUT CRYSTAL FOUNT

POLISHED BRASS FOUNT AND REEDED PILLAR WITH BLACK BASE

DUPLEX LAMPS

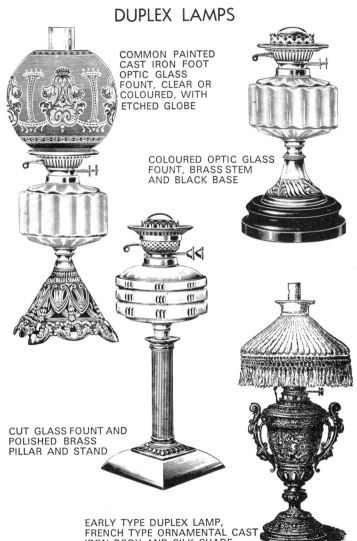

COMMON PAINTED
CAST IRON FOOT
OPTIC GLASS
FOUNT, CLEAR OR
COLOURED, WITH
ETCHED GLOBE

COLOURED OPTIC GLASS
FOUNT, BRASS STEM
AND BLACK BASE

CUT GLASS FOUNT AND
POLISHED BRASS
PILLAR AND STAND

EARLY TYPE DUPLEX LAMP,
FRENCH TYPE ORNAMENTAL CAST
IRON BODY AND SILK SHADE

KOSMOS LAMPS

POLISHED BRASS WITH
10''' KOSMOS BURNER &
7½'' OPAL SHADE

POLISHED BRASS
WITH 6''' KOSMOS
BURNER

NICKEL PLATED
WITH 6''' KOSMOS
BURNER

POLISHED BRASS WITH
10''' KOSMOS BURNER

NICKEL PLATED BRASS
WITH 10''' KOSMOS BURNER

THE KOSMOS BURNER WAS PRODUCED IN GREAT VOLUME AND IN SEVEN SIZES. THOUGH THE BURNER WAS TUBULAR IT TOOK A FLAT WICK AND AT TIMES OFFERED PROBLEMS IN RE-WICKING. THE CHIMNEYS WERE MADE IN TWO LENGTHS, THE SHORTER FOR HAND LAMPS AND THE TALLER FOR TABLE LAMPS

KOSMOS BURNERS:-
6'''—1⅚'' CHIMNEY FITTING
8'''—1⁷⁄₁₆'' ,, ,,
10'''—1½'' ,, ,,
12'''—1¾'' CHIMNEY FITTING
14'''—2'' ,, ,,
16'''—2¼'' ,, ,,
18'''—2⁷⁄₁₆'' ,, ,,

THE 6''' AND 10''' SIZES ARE THE MOST COMMON.

WIZARD AND SIMILAR TABLE LAMPS

15''' WIZARD POLISHED
BRASS WITH 7½''
OPAL VESTA SHADE

15''' MIKADO POLISHED
BRASS WITH 7½''
OPAL VESTA SHADE

14''' ORION, POLISHED
BRASS WITH 7½''
OPAL SHADE

15''' MIKADO
POLISHED BRASS
& COPPER

CENTRAL DRAUGHT LAMPS

VERITAS, MADE IN 20''' (50 cp)
& 30''' (100 cp). THE MOST
POPULAR LAMP OF
THE VICTORIAN ERA

14''' ORION & 16''' HELIOS
BRASS FOUNT FOR
BRACKET, TABLE OR
HANGING LAMPS

20''' (50 cp) VERITAS WITH
PILLAR OF GREEN
BRAZILIAN MARBLE,
POLISHED BRASS FOUNT
AND GILT FITTINGS.

20''' INTERNATIONAL
POLISHED BRASS
MADE BY MATTHIAS
JACKSON OF
MANCHESTER

16''' HELIOS WITH
POLISHED BRASS
FOUNT
AND STAND WITH
MANOGRAPHY SHADE

QUEENS READING LAMPS

QUEENS READING LAMP FOR
COLZA OIL WITH 12''' BURNER
AND 6'' OPAL SHADE
POLISHED BRASS OR
NICKEL PLATED

QUEENS READING LAMP
FOR COLZA OIL

ORIGINALLY DESIGNED FOR
COLZA OIL WITH ITS GRAVITY
FED BURNER, IT WAS
EVENTUALLY MADE FOR
BOTH COLZA AND PETROLEUM.
LARGE QUANTITIES OF THESE
LAMPS STILL SURVIVE AND
FLATTERING IMITATIONS FOR
ELECTRICITY ARE POPULAR.
SHADES WERE WHITE OPAL
OR GREEN WITH WHITE
LINING

QUEENS READING LAMP FOR
PETROLEUM. 14''' BURNER AND
7'' OPAL SHADE. POLISHED
BRASS OR NICKEL PLATED

SPARE PARTS LISTED FOR
THESE LAMPS WERE TIN
BURNER TUBES, WICK HOLDERS,
CHIMNEY HOLDERS & DRIP CUPS

STANDARD LAMPS

STANDARD LAMPS GENERALLY FITTED WITH 20‴ (50 cp) CENTRAL DRAUGHT FOUNTS SUCH AS VERITAS, WERE USUALLY TELESCOPIC TO PROVIDE A MEASURE OF HEIGHT ADJUSTMENT. STANDARDS MADE OF BRASS, WROUGHT IRON, OCCASIONALLY WOOD, FREQUENTLY CARRIED LARGE FANCY SHADES OF SILK. FAMOS & SIMILAR INCANDESCENT LAMPS WERE OFFERED AS AN ALTERNATIVE TO THE CENTRAL DRAUGHT LAMPS.

WROUGHT IRON, COPPER FITTINGS, IMITATION ONYX TABLE. TELESCOPIC

WOODEN STANDARD, BLACK LACQUERED WITH ORIENTAL DESIGN & SILK SHADE. NOT TELESCOPIC

BRASS STANDARD POLISHED FINISH, OXY COPPER OR OXY SILVER. TELESCOPIC

HARP LAMPS

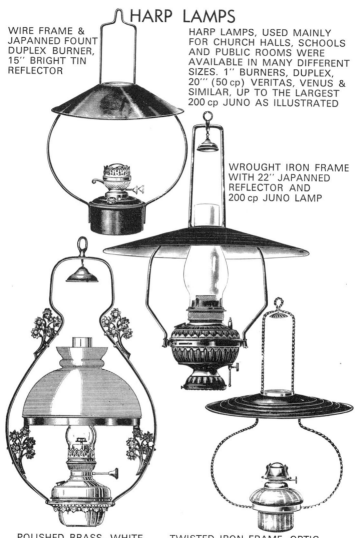

WIRE FRAME & JAPANNED FOUNT DUPLEX BURNER, 15" BRIGHT TIN REFLECTOR

HARP LAMPS, USED MAINLY FOR CHURCH HALLS, SCHOOLS AND PUBLIC ROOMS WERE AVAILABLE IN MANY DIFFERENT SIZES. 1" BURNERS, DUPLEX, 20''' (50 cp) VERITAS, VENUS & SIMILAR, UP TO THE LARGEST 200 cp JUNO AS ILLUSTRATED

WROUGHT IRON FRAME WITH 22" JAPANNED REFLECTOR AND 200 cp JUNO LAMP

POLISHED BRASS, WHITE OPAL SHADE AND 20''' (50 cp) VENUS LAMP

TWISTED IRON FRAME, OPTIC GLASS FOUNT, COMET OR SLIP BURNER, 15" JAPANNED REFLECTOR

SUSPENSION LAMPS

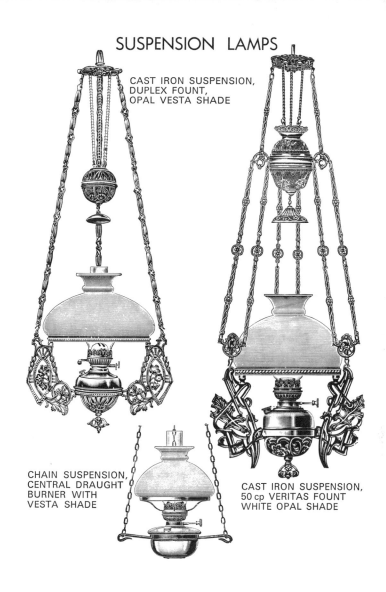

CAST IRON SUSPENSION,
DUPLEX FOUNT,
OPAL VESTA SHADE

CHAIN SUSPENSION,
CENTRAL DRAUGHT
BURNER WITH
VESTA SHADE

CAST IRON SUSPENSION,
50 cp VERITAS FOUNT
WHITE OPAL SHADE

VESTIBULE LAMPS

OXIDISED COPPER
ROSE SHADED PANELS
WITH PIXIE BURNER

ROSE SHADED GLASS,
PLATED FRAME AND
6''' KOSMOS BURNER

CATHEDRAL GLASS
AND SLIP BURNER

PLATED FRAME WITH
ORANGE SHADED PANELS
AND 10''' KOSMOS BURNER

TINTED MANOGRAPHY
GLOBE, BRASS FITTINGS
& FOUNT FITTED WITH
$\frac{3}{4}$'' SLIP BURNER

SWING BRACKET LAMPS

GLASS FOUNT WITH
MIKADO BURNER AND
SANDBLAST
GLOBE

CARAVAN TYPE, BRASS
WITH DUPLEX BURNER
& MANOGRAPHY GLOBE

COPPER BRONZED,
SILVERED GLASS
REFLECTOR, BRASS
15'''MIKADO LAMP

BRASS BRACKET, GLASS
FOUNT, DUPLEX BURNER,
TULIP MANOGRAPHY GLOBE

WITH 20'''
VERITAS
FOUNT

SWING BRACKET LAMPS WERE USED IN
CARAVANS, HALLS & LANDINGS ETC. THE
BRACKETS WERE MADE OF POLISHED BRASS,
WROUGHT IRON OR CAST IRON. THE LAMPS
WERE AVAILABLE IN ALL SIZES OF BURNERS,
1'' FLAT WICK, DUPLEX AND 15'''MIKADO OR
WIZARD. WHERE MORE LIGHT WAS NEEDED
BRACKETS WERE FITTED WITH 20''' (50 cp)
CENTRAL DRAUGHT LAMPS SUCH AS VERITAS

GLASS DUPLEX
FOUNT AND
MANOGRAPHY
GLOBE

PIANO LAMPS

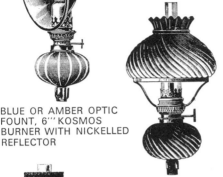

SATIN MOULDED,
ROSE SHADED WITH
6''' KOSMOS BURNER

BLUE OR AMBER OPTIC
FOUNT, 6''' KOSMOS
BURNER WITH NICKELLED
REFLECTOR

BLUE OR AMBER OPTIC
FOUNT, OPAL SHADE.
AND 6''' KOSMOS
BURNER

CUT CRYSTAL FOUNT
SILK SHADE AND 6'''
KOSMOS BURNER

POLISHED BRASS
WITH 10'''
KOSMOS BURNER
REFLECTOR AND
WEIGHTED BASE

BRASS WITH 10''' KOSMOS
BURNER AND NICKEL
PLATED REFLECTOR

PIANO LAMPS ARE FITTED WITH
SPRING TOE TO FIT THE CANDLE
SCONCE. OTHER TYPES SCREW
DIRECT TO THE PIANO CASE OR
HAVE A WEIGHTED BASE AND
SWIVEL BRACKET

HAND LAMPS AND WALL BACK LAMPS

GEM ARCTIC

WITH COMET, EUREKA, STAR OR QUEEN ANNE BURNERS IN $\frac{1}{2}''$, $\frac{3}{4}''$ & 1'' WICK SIZES. IN POLISHED BRASS OR OPTIC OR CRYSTAL GLASS. CHIMNEY FITTINGS, 2'', $2\frac{1}{2}''$ & 3'', BULGE OR TRAM COMET SHAPE

POLISHED BRASS WITH $\frac{3}{4}''$ OR 1'' SLIP BURNER TAKING SHORT BULGE CHIMNEY $1\frac{3}{4}''$ OR $2\frac{1}{16}''$ FITTING

GEM PRONG, SMALLEST SIZE IN FLAT WICK HAND LAMPS, TAKING A GEM PINE CHIMNEY WITH $1\frac{5}{8}''$ FITTING

KAFFIR CHIMNEYLESS STUFFED FOR BENZOLINE, UNSTUFFED FOR PARAFFIN

CIRCULAR WICK NIGHT LIGHT KELLY, LUNA, DON, PIXIE, ETC. MADE IN WALL AND HAND LAMP VERSIONS

JAPANNED BODY, MIRROR REFLECTOR, FITTED WITH COMMON DUPLEX BURNER

JAPANNED BODY, HEAVILY TINNED OR PLATED REFLECTOR FITTED WITH COMMON DUPLEX BURNER

BACK LAMPS WERE ALSO MADE WITH $\frac{3}{4}''$ AND 1'' SLIP BURNERS AND 50 cp OR 100 cp VERITAS

INCANDESCENT LAMPS

FAMOS NON-PRESSURE TYPE
BY FALKS. 90 AND 120 cp

TILLEY SHORT MODEL No. 136
TALL MODEL No. 106
PRESSURE TYPE
PARAFFIN

COLEMAN COMBINATION
OF LAMP & LANTERN
AVAILABLE FOR PETROL OR
PARAFFIN. PRESSURE TYPE

ALADDIN
NON-PRESSURE
TYPES.
EARLY MODELS WITH
PLAIN CHIMNEY,
LATER WITH LOXON
MANTLE AND CHIMNEY

NOVA PETROL MODEL
AN EARLY CONTINENTAL
LAMP. PRESSURE TYPE

PRESSURE-TYPE LANTERNS WERE WIDELY USED, MADE
MAINLY BY TILLEY, BI-ALADDIN, COLEMAN, AND PRIMUS.
MANY MODELS ARE STILL IN PRODUCTION.

CHURCH LAMPS

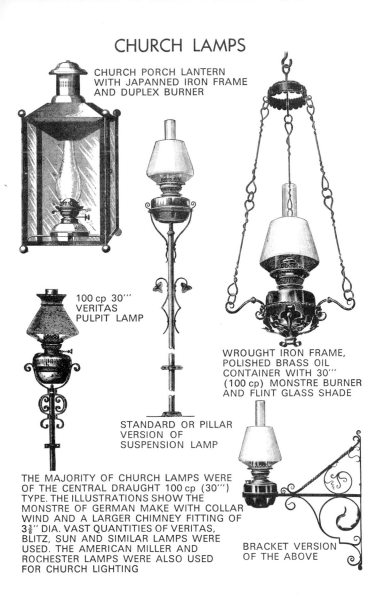

CHURCH PORCH LANTERN WITH JAPANNED IRON FRAME AND DUPLEX BURNER

100 cp 30'''
VERITAS
PULPIT LAMP

WROUGHT IRON FRAME, POLISHED BRASS OIL CONTAINER WITH 30''' (100 cp) MONSTRE BURNER AND FLINT GLASS SHADE

STANDARD OR PILLAR VERSION OF SUSPENSION LAMP

THE MAJORITY OF CHURCH LAMPS WERE OF THE CENTRAL DRAUGHT 100 cp (30''') TYPE. THE ILLUSTRATIONS SHOW THE MONSTRE OF GERMAN MAKE WITH COLLAR WIND AND A LARGER CHIMNEY FITTING OF $3\frac{3}{8}''$ DIA. VAST QUANTITIES OF VERITAS, BLITZ, SUN AND SIMILAR LAMPS WERE USED. THE AMERICAN MILLER AND ROCHESTER LAMPS WERE ALSO USED FOR CHURCH LIGHTING

BRACKET VERSION OF THE ABOVE

MARINE LAMPS

STERN

ANCHOR

MASTHEAD
(CLEAR)

SIDE,
STARBOARD
(GREEN)
OR PORT (RED)

TRICOLOUR RELIEVING
LAMP JAPANNED
WITH COLZA BURNER

GIMBAL LAMP
FOR CABINS

TRICOLOUR
YACHT LAMP

HAND MORSE
LAMP FOR OIL

LAMP WITH
CONE FOR
NAVIGATION
LIGHTS

SUNDRY LAMPS AND LANTERNS

TYPICAL COLD BLAST LANTERN TYPE IDENTIFIED BY LARGE AIR MIXING DOME $\frac{5}{8}$'' or 1'' WICK

TRACTION ENGINE LAMP, HEAVY DUTY $\frac{5}{8}$'', $\frac{3}{4}$'' OR 1'' WICK

GUARDS SIGNALLING LAMP. TRICOLOUR SLIDE WITH $\frac{3}{4}$'' COLZA BURNER

BULLS EYE LANTERN $6\frac{1}{2}$'', $7\frac{1}{4}$'' & 8'' HIGH ALSO WITH TRICOLOUR SLIDE

CYCLE LAMP WITH CLEAR OR BULLS EYE LENS. RUBY GLASS FOR REAR LAMP COLZA BURNER $\frac{5}{8}$'' OR $\frac{3}{4}$'' WICK SIZE, 7 HOUR CAPACITY

TYPICAL HOT BLAST LANTERN $\frac{5}{8}$'' WICK SIZE

DOMESTIC LANTERN MADE OF BRASS, $\frac{1}{2}$'' BURNER

COMMON CART LAMP JAPANNED, $\frac{5}{8}$'', $\frac{3}{4}$'' & 1'' WICK

OMNIBUS LAMP USED BY HORSE DRAWN OMNIBUSES FOR COLZA OIL

LAMP SUNDRIES

MICA CHIMNEY TOPS FOR CEILING PROTECTION

BRASS CEILING HOOK

WICK SCISSORS

POLISHED BRASS
from 4¾˝ to 12˝

ENAMELLED STEEL
6˝ to 12˝

CLEAR GLASS 6˝ to 12˝

SUSPENSION CHAIN

SMOKE BELLS

COLLARS

GEM OR ½˝ — 35 mm outside diameter
⅝˝ OR ¾˝ — 46 mm or 58 mm do
  ⅞˝ — 60 or 65 mm do
1˝ OR 10˝ — 58 or 65 mm do
DUPLEX SCREW — 65 mm do
DUPLEX BAYONET — 68 mm do

SHADE RINGS
6˝ KOSMOS — 5¾˝
10˝ „ — 7⅞˝
DUPLEX
  7½˝ & 9½˝
20˝ BURNERS
100 cp Lamps — 10˝ & 11˝
TO FIT 4˝ GALLERY — 9½˝, 10˝ & 11˝

3 WAY STRAP BASKET
FOR 5½˝ FOUNT
No 10 SCREW FITTING

BALANCE PULLEY
CAST IRON OR BRASS
IN VARIOUS WEIGHTS

COLLAR FOR CONVERTING
BAYONET TO SCREW
FITTING IN DUPLEX

FOUNT SOCKET
No 7 OR No 10
SCREW FITTING

GALLERY 3˝ OR 4˝ FITTING
FOR GLOBES

BURNER PARTS, (FLAME SPREADERS OR DIFFUSERS)

A FEW OF THE
MORE POPULAR
PATTERNS

20˝
EXCELLENTA
AND INVICTA

DEFRIES
1 and 2

VENUS
20˝ & 30˝

VERITAS
20˝ & 30˝

SUN 30˝
(Sherwood)

SUPERBA,
HELIOS,
PROGRESS
12˝, 14˝, 16˝

WIZARD 15˝
(NEW)

WONDER

PEOPLES

GLOBE VULCAN
16˝, 18˝, 24˝

WIZARD &
MIKADO (OLD)
15˝

HELIOS 20˝

MATADOR

SUNLIGHT

TOREX
2 & 3

THERMIDOR
& BELGE
14˝, 20˝, 30˝

PIN PATTERN
FOR CHARMER
& POPULAR 15˝

COURT
16˝, 20˝
& 30˝

CHAMPION

EDEN, EDINA,
KRONOS,
CHALLENGE

MIKADO
(NEW) 15˝
ORION 14˝
HELIOS 16˝
VICEROY
CORONATION

THE FLAME SPREADER OR DIFFUSER IS AN ESSENTIAL PART OF THE CENTRAL DRAUGHT BURNER.
BY ITS FUNCTION IT NEEDS REPLACEMENT FROM TIME TO TIME AND FREQUENTLY LAMPS ARE
FOUND WITH THEIR SPREADERS MISSING OR BROKEN

AS THE SPREADERS ARE NOW UNOBTAINABLE, THE ILLUSTRATIONS MAY BE OF ASSISTANCE IN
IDENTIFYING BROKEN SPECIMENS WITH A VIEW TO REPAIRING OR REPLACING THEM

GLOBES

7½" x 4" OR 6½" x 3"
OPAL OR OPAL & FLINT

7½" x 4"
SANDBLAST

SHERWOODS
MAGIC
NIGHT LIGHT
GLOBE

SHERWOODS
ELVELIT
NIGHT LIGHT
GLOBE

7½" x 4" MANOGRAPHY
ETCHED, TINTED ROSE, GREEN,
YELLOW OR BLUE

CLEAR OR OPAL
FOR PIXIE, LUNA
DON & KELLY LAMPS

4" FITTING CLEAR OR
TINTED ETCHED
MANOGRAPHY

4" FITTING, TULIP SHAPE
TINTED OPTIC

4" OR 3" FITTING
TINTED ETCHED MANOGRAPHY
TULIP SHAPE

7½" x 4" OPAL
FLANGE FITTING
FOR SALOON AND
CABIN LAMPS

SHADES AND GLASSWARE

WHITE
OPAL
GLASS

LARGE DOME
9¼", 10", 11", 11¾", 12", 13", 13¾", 14",
15¾", 17¾".

TAPER
9", 10", 11",   11¾",   13¾",   15¾", 17¾".

WHITE OPAL FOR
EARLY TYPE TILLEY

WHITE OPAL PARIS SHAPE
DOMED SHADE WITH PLAIN
OR CRIMPED TOP.
8½" x 4", 10" x 4"

WHITE OPAL FOR INCANDESCENT LAMPS 9¼"

WHITE OPAL FOR MILLER
No. 0-6", No. 1-7", No. 2-10" No. 3-14"

WHITE OPAL OR GREEN CASED
FOR QUEENS READING LAMP
5", 5½", 6", 7", 7½".

WHITE OPAL OR GREEN CASED
VESTA SHAPE, THE MOST POPULAR
STYLE OF GLASS SHADE
FOR KOSMOS 6"-5⅜", 8"-5⅜",
"   "   10"-7⅜", 14"-9¼".
ALSO FOR GENERAL USE 11", 11¾", 13", 13¾", 15¾",

JUGEND
WHITE OPAL OR GREEN CASED 7¼" OR 9¼".

SHIP'S CONE GLASS
4⅞" TOP -   1⅞" FITTING

39

BURNERS

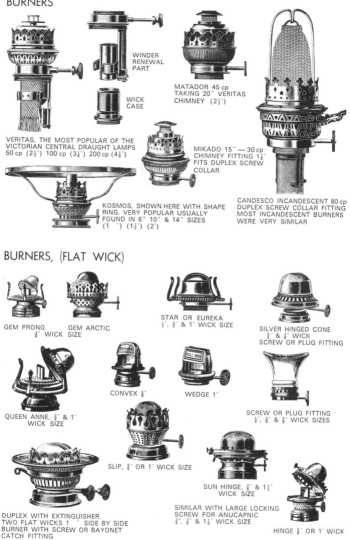

WINDER RENEWAL PART

WICK CASE

VERITAS, THE MOST POPULAR OF THE VICTORIAN CENTRAL DRAUGHT LAMPS 50 cp (2½") 100 cp (3¼") 200 cp (4¼")

MATADOR 45 cp TAKING 20''' VERITAS CHIMNEY (2½")

MIKADO 15''' — 30 cp. CHIMNEY FITTING 1½" FITS DUPLEX SCREW COLLAR

KOSMOS, SHOWN HERE WITH SHAPE RING. VERY POPULAR USUALLY FOUND IN 6''' 10''' & 14''' SIZES (1''') (1½") (2")

CANDESCO INCANDESCENT 80 cp DUPLEX SCREW COLLAR FITTING MOST INCANDESCENT BURNERS WERE VERY SIMILAR

BURNERS, (FLAT WICK)

GEM PRONG ⅞" WICK

GEM ARCTIC SIZE

STAR OR EUREKA ½", ¾" & 1" WICK SIZE

SILVER HINGED CONE ⅝" & ⅞" WICK SCREW OR PLUG FITTING

QUEEN ANNE, ¾" & 1" WICK SIZE

CONVEX ⅝"

WEDGE 1"

SCREW OR PLUG FITTING ¼", ⅜" & ⅝" WICK SIZES

SLIP, ¾" OR 1" WICK SIZE

DUPLEX WITH EXTINGUISHER. TWO FLAT WICKS 1''' SIDE BY SIDE BURNER WITH SCREW OR BAYONET CATCH FITTING

SUN HINGE, ⅞" & 1½" WICK SIZE

SIMILAR WITH LARGE LOCKING SCREW FOR ANUCAPNIC ¾", ⅞" & 1¼" WICK SIZE

HINGE ⅞" OR 1" WICK

LAMP CHIMNEYS

		Burner	Length	Fitting	
ARIEL		16'''	10⅜"	2⅛"	SUITABLE FOR ARIEL, HELIOS, ORBIT, RADIANT MINERVA PERFECTION, SOUTHWARK
		20'''	10½"	2½"	ARIEL, JUNO, HESPER, NATIONAL & VENUS
		30'''	12½"	3"	JUNO, HESPER, NATIONAL & VENUS
BLITZ		20'''	11½"	2½"	BLITZ, PREMIER & IMPERIAL
		30'''	12½"	3"	do do do
BELGE		30 cp	9½"	1⅞"	ALSO CORONATION
		50 cp	10½"	2½"	ALSO 60 cp GRANVILLE BELGE & ANNULAR
		100 cp	12½"	3"	
CLARISSA		15'''	9½"	2⅛"	CLARISSA MATADOR & REFORM WONDER
		20'''	10¾"	2½"	do do do
		30'''	12¾"	3 1/16"	do do do
CILAXO	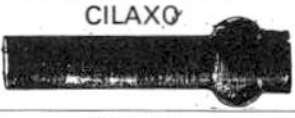	20'''	11"	2½"	CILAXO, HELIOS, SUNRISE
COURT		16'''	9½"	2 1/16"	
		20'''	10½"	2 9/16"	COURT OR EAGLE
		30'''	12¾"	3 1/16"	
OLD DEFRIES	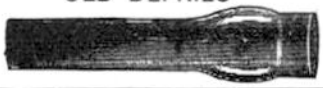	No 1	11⅝"	2⅜"	NEW DEFRIES 9⅞" LONG
		No 2	12⅜"	2⅝"	NEW DEFRIES 11½" LONG
		No 3	13⅝"	3 1/16"	
MONSTRE	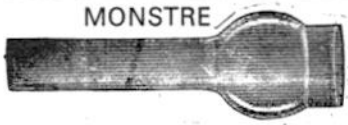	30'''	13½"	3⅜"	FOR COLLAR WIND CHURCH LAMPS
DEFRIES		No 10	8¼"	1 5/16"	
		No 15	9¾"	1½"	
		No 20	11"	2 1/16"	
KOSMOS		6'''	7"	1 5/16"	
		8'''	7"	1 7/16"	LONG TYPE 9"
		10'''	9"	1½"	LONG TYPE 10"
		12'''	10"	1¾"	
		14'''	10½"	2"	
		16'''	11"	2¼"	
		18'''	11"	2 7/16"	
WIZARD		10'''	8¼"	1⅜"	ALSO PEOPLES & POPULAR
		15'''	10¼"	1⅞"	ALSO 15''' OPHIR
		16'''	10½"	2⅛"	ALSO 16''' ODIN
		20'''	10½"	2½"	ALSO 25''' ODIN
MIKADO		15'''	9¾"	1⅞"	ALSO PEOPLES, POPULAR REFORM & CHARMER
ORION		14'''	9"	1⅞"	ALSO RADIANT, PROGRESS BRITELITE, SOUTHWARK & SUPERBA
K & T SUN		14'''	9½"	2⅛"	
		20'''	11¼"	2½"	
		30'''	13¼"	3⅜"	30''' CHIMNEY IS SLIGHTLY WAISTED
ENGLISH SUN		15'''	9½"	2 1/16"	
		20'''	11¼"	2½"	
		30'''	13½"	3⅜"	
VERITAS		20'''-50cp	10½"	2½"	
		30'''-100cp	12½"	3⅛"	
		60'''-200cp	12"	4¼"	
QUEENS READING		12'''	10"	1¾"	SIMILAR SHAPE FOR MITRAILLEUSE
		14'''	10¼"	1⅞"	12 PIPE—12"—2½"
		18'''	10½"	2 1/16"	16 ,, —12"—2½"
					20 ,, —13"—3⅛"
VICTORIA	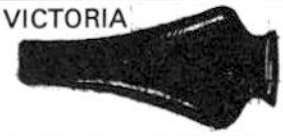	No 8	10"	3"	
		No 9	11"	3⅛"	

LAMP CHIMNEYS

	Burner		Length	Fitting	
INCANDESCENT 	FAMOS				THE INCANDESCENT GROUP TOOK SIMILAR SHAPE CHIMNEYS WITH FITTINGS AS SHOWN
	ALADDIN II		12½"	2⅝"	
	RARELITE				
	LITENITE		13"	2 9/16"	
	SUNLIGHT		12½"	2 9/16"	
	NUSUNLITE		12½"	2½"	
	CANDESCO				EXCEPT LUCISCA NEW FUMAR, PIFCO CHALLENGE & KRONOS WHICH TOOK A STRAIGHT CHIMNEY 12¾" x 2⅛"
	ESSO				
	EDINA				
	ARRO				
	MORLITE		12½"	2⅛"	
VULCAN 	14‴ VULCAN		10½"	2"	
	16‴ ,,		11⅝"	2¼"	
	18‴ ,,		12"	2⅜"	
	24‴ ,,		12¼"	2¾"	
	30‴ ,,		13"	3⅛"	
	50‴ ,,		13¼"	3⅞"	
WRIGHT & BUTLER UNION 	No. 0 UNION		7¼"	1½"	
	No. 1 ,,		8⅜"	2"	
	No. 2 ,,		9½"	2⅝"	
	No. 10 ,,		12"	3 15/16"	
	No. 0 MILLER		7¼"	1½"	ALSO FOR ROCHESTER
	No. 1 ,,		8¼"	2"	
	No. 2 ,,		9"	2⅝"	
	No. 2 ,, LONG		10"	2⅝"	
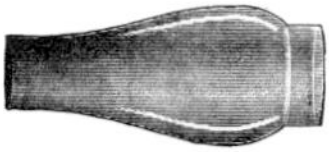	No. 3 MILLER				
	No. 10 ROCHESTER				
	200 cp JUNO		12½"	4"	
	HESPERUS		9½"	3⅛"	
	45 cp HINKS		11"	2½"	
	80 cp HINKS		11"	2 15/16"	
	NEW SILBER 1		11¾"	3"	
	,, ,, 2		10¾"	2½"	
	14‴ LIGHTHOUSE		10½"	2"	
	MARVEL 10‴		10"	1⅞"	ALSO SUNBEAM TRIUMPH & DAYLIGHT IN SAME SIZES & FITTINGS
	,, 15‴		11¾"	2 5/16"	
	,, 20‴		12"	2½"	
	,, 30‴		14¼"	2⅞"	
BULGE SLIP 	BULGE SLIP				
	6 SHORT	½"	7"	1½"	
	8 SHORT	¾"	7"	1¾"	
	8 LONG	¾"	10"	1¾"	
	10 SHORT	1"	7"	2 1/16"	
	10 LONG	1"	10⅜"	2 1/16"	
	14 LONG	1½"	11"	2¾"	THIS GROUP OF CHIMNEYS IS TO FIT THE RANGE OF SLIP BURNERS. THE BULGE TYPE IS FOR HAND LAMPS IN THE SHORT STYLE AND THE LONG FOR TABLE LAMPS. THE STRAIGHT AND THE OVAL SHAPES ARE FOR WALL AND BACK LAMPS WHERE SPACE IS RESTRICTED.
OVAL SLIP 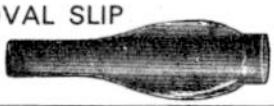	No. 8	¾"	9¼"	1¾"	
	No. 10	1"	10"	2 1/16"	
ROWATTS 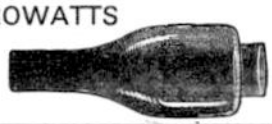	No. 8	¾"	9¼"	1¾"	
	No. 10	1"	9⅞"	2 1/16"	
STRAIGHT SLIP 	No 5 SHORT	½"	6"	1¼"	
	No 8 SHORT	¾"	7⅜"	1¾"	
	No 8 LONG	¾"	9"	1¾"	
	No 10 SHORT	1"	7½"	2 1/16"	
	No 10 LONG	1"	10½"	2 1/16"	
DUPLEX 	STANDARD DUPLEX				THE DUPLEX CHIMNEY IS OVAL IN ITS STANDARD FORM, AND SHOULD BE FITTED WITH THE BULGE PARALLEL TO THE WICKS
	SHORT	1 1/16"	10"	2½"	
			8"	2½"	
	ROUND		10"	2½"	
TRIPLEX 	TRIPLEX		11"	3⅛"	

LAMP CHIMNEYS

		Burner	Length	Fitting	
	PARAGON & TIGER	PARAGON TIGER	10½" 10½"	2⅜" 2⅝"	
	BIJOU	½"	6½"	1¾"	for HINKS NIGHT LIGHT
	BULGE BIJOU	½"	6"	1¾"	for ALLISONS LAMP
	DUPLEX BIJOU	¼"	7⅛"	1¾"	for TWIN WICK ¼" HAND LAMP
	BULGE COMET	⅜" ⅝" ⅞"	6½" 7½" 7¾"	2 1/16" 2½" 3"	FOR QUEEN ANNE OR EUREKA BURNERS ALSO CHIMNEYS IN OVAL SHAPE & STRAIGHT PATTERN WERE USED SIMILAR B.O.T. PATTERN AND SHIPS SHORT COMET
	TRAM COMET	⅜" ⅝" ⅞"	6" 6¼" 7¼"	2 1/16" 2½" 3"	FOR QUEEN ANNE, EUREKA & SIMILAR BURNERS
	SUN PINE	⅝" ⅞" ⅞"	8½" 9" 9"	2½" 3" 3"	ALSO SHORT 6½" " " 7½" 5" LARGE BULGE FOR EUREKA & QUEEN ANNE BURNER
	GEM PINE	GEM	4¾" 5¼"	1⅝" 1⅝"	ALSO OVAL & PEARL TOP TYPES
		STELLA MAGIC LANTERN 2''' 3''' 5''' 8'''	5" 3⅝" 3¾" 5¼" 9¾"	1½" 1 5/16" 1 5/16" 1½" 1 11/16"	ALSO A NUTMEG CHIMNEY OF SIMILAR SHAPE 3⅝" x 1⅛"
	FLANGE	HINGE ⅝" HINGE ⅞" HINGE 1¼"	5" 5" 5½"	1⅝" 2 1/16" 2¼"	ALSO LONG 6" ALSO LONG 6½" ALSO LONG 7½"
	WONDER	ORIGINAL WONDER IMPROVED 8''' 10'''	7¾" 8½" 8¾"	1½" 1¼" 1½"	ALSO A STRAIGHT CHIMNEY 7¾" x 1½"
	SHIP CONE	STANDARD YACHT	4½" 3½"	1⅞" 1¾"	

BIBLIOGRAPHY

Iron and Brass Implements of the English House; J. Seymour Lindsay; Medici, London, 1927.

Period Lighting Fixtures; Mr. and Mrs. G. Glen Gould; Dodd, Mead & Co., New York, 1928.

A Short History of Lighting; W. T. O'Dea; Science Museum (HMSO).

The Story of Light; Jeannette Eaton; Harper & Bros., New York, 1928.

The Story of the Lamp; F. W. Robins, Oxford University Press, 1939.

For the student or collector of Victorian lamps tables of wick and chimney sizes may be of great value. This information is not readily available elsewhere, particularly as the old catalogues are rare and almost impossible to acquire or even borrow.

The symbol ‴, referred to as 'line', should be explained. For comparison a 20‴ lamp was rated as 50 candlepower and a 30‴ as 100 candlepower, these lamps being of central draught design and taking circular wicks. The system of line measurement is of German origin and was widely adopted by manufacturers in other countries. There is no exact conversion of line to chimney dimensions or wick sizes.

The following table lists the principal chimneys and globes and gives their dimensions and fittings. The list is complete as far as is possible and alternative names are given where they are known. In some cases chimneys are interchangeable and a conversion table is given showing the common fittings, always provided that the shape of the chimney will suit the draught design of the burner.

Principal Lamp Chimneys by Base Diameters

$1\frac{1}{8}''$	Nutmeg
$1\frac{3}{16}''$	1‴ Lilliput
$1\frac{1}{4}''$	Improved Wonder
$1\frac{5}{16}''$	10 Defries, 3‴ Lantern, 6‴ Kosmos
$1\frac{3}{8}''$	10‴ Wizard
$1\frac{7}{16}''$	8‴ Kosmos
$1\frac{1}{2}''$	10‴ Securitas, Original Wonder, 15 Defries, 0 Miller, 0 Rochester, 0 Union, 1 Thermidor, 6 Slip, 5‴ Lantern, Stella, 10‴ Kosmos
$1\frac{9}{16}''$	2 Thermidor
$1\frac{5}{8}''$	Gem
$1\frac{3}{4}''$	8 Bulge, Bijou, Queens 12‴, Kosmos 12‴
$1\frac{7}{8}''$	15‴ Wizard, 15‴ Mikado, 15‴ Ophir, 14‴ Securitas, 30 c.p. Belge, 15‴ Charmer, 15‴ Reform, 15‴ Popular, 15‴ Peoples, Coronation, 10 Marvel, 10 Sunbeam, 10 Triumph, 10 Daylight, 14‴ Orion, 14‴ Radiant, 14‴ Progress, 14‴ Britelite, 14‴ Southwark, 14‴ Superba, 14‴ Queens
$2''$	14‴ Lighthouse, 1 Miller, 1 Rochester, 1 Union, 4 Silber, 14‴ Vulcan, 14‴ Kosmos
$2\frac{1}{16}''$	16‴ Court, 16‴ Eagle, 20 Defries, 15‴ English Sun, 15‴ Viceroy, 18‴ Queens, 10 Bulge or Slip, Eureka, Comet, Queen Anne, Tram

$2\frac{1}{8}''$	16''' Wizard, 16''' Ariel, 16''' Helios, 16''' Orbit, 16''' Minerva, 16''' Radiant, 16''' Perfection, 18''' Southwark, 15''' Clarissa, Candesco, Esso, Edina, Arro, Morelite, Lucisca, New Fumar, Pifco, Challenge, Kronos, 16''' Odin, 15''' Matador, 15''' Reform Wonder
$2\frac{1}{4}''$	16''' Vulcan, 16''' Kosmos
$2\frac{5}{16}''$	15''' Marvel, 15''' Sunbeam, 15''' Triumph, 15''' Daylight
$2\frac{3}{8}''$	1 New and Old Defries, 18''' Vulcan, Paragon
$2\frac{7}{16}''$	18''' Kosmos
$2\frac{1}{2}''$	60 c.p. Granville Belge, 12 p. Mitrailleuse, 50 c.p. Belge, 2 Silber, 54 c.p. Annular, 45 c.p. Hinks, Nusunlite, Duplex, Comet or Tram. All 20'''—Wizard, Ariel, Juno, Hesper, National, Venus, Blitz, Imperial, Premier, Clarissa, Matador, Cilaxo, Helios, Sunrise, Marvel, Sunbeam, Triumph, Daylight, English Sun, Radiant, Veritas, Sun Pine, Odin
$2\frac{9}{16}''$	20''' Court, 20''' Eagle, Sunlight, Rarelite, Litenite
$2\frac{5}{8}''$	2 Miller, 2 Rochester, 2 Union, 2 New and Old Defries, Famos, 11 Aladdin
$2\frac{3}{4}''$	24''' Vulcan, 14 Slip or Bulge
$2\frac{7}{8}''$	30''' Marvel, 30''' Triumph, 30''' Sunbeam, 30''' Daylight, 5 Anucapnic
$2\frac{15}{16}''$	80 Hinks
$3''$	All 30'''—Juno, Hesper, National, Venus, Blitz, Imperial, Premier, 100 c.p. Belge, 1 Silber, Comet, Sun Pine, Victoria 8
$3\frac{1}{16}''$	All 30'''—Clarissa, Matador, Court, Eagle, 3 Old Defries
$3\frac{1}{8}''$	30''' Veritas, 30''' Vulcan, Triplex, Victoria 9, 20 c.p. Mitrailleuse, 7 Anucapnic, Hesperus
$3\frac{3}{8}''$	30''' Monstre, 30''' English Sun
$3\frac{1}{2}''$	9 Anucapnic
$3\frac{3}{4}''$	12 Anucapnic
$3\frac{7}{8}''$	50''' Vulcan
$3\frac{15}{16}''$	10 Union
$4''$	3 Miller, 3 Rochester, 200 c.p. Juno
$4\frac{1}{4}''$	60''' Veritas

Wicks

The details of popular wick sizes are given for reference purposes. As much of this information is not readily available elsewhere a table of comparisons is given on page 47, showing alternatives if the original wick is unobtainable.

Flat wick sizes: $\frac{1}{4}''$, $\frac{5}{16}''$, $\frac{3}{8}''$, $\frac{7}{16}''$, $\frac{1}{2}''$, $\frac{5}{8}''$, $\frac{11}{16}''$, $\frac{3}{4}''$, $\frac{7}{8}''$, 1'', $1\frac{1}{16}''$, $1\frac{1}{4}''$, $1\frac{1}{2}''$.

Kosmos: 6'''—$1\frac{3}{8}''$, 8'''—$1\frac{5}{8}''$, 10'''—$1\frac{15}{16}''$, 12'''—$2\frac{1}{4}''$, 14'''—$2\frac{5}{8}''$.

Anucapnic: $\frac{5}{8}''$, $\frac{3}{4}''$, $\frac{7}{8}''$, $1\frac{1}{16}''$, $1\frac{3}{8}''$.

Eden, Edina or Challenge: 3'' x 9''.

Candesco (old) and New Fumar: $2\frac{3}{4}'' \times 8\frac{3}{4}''$.
Matador: $20''' - 3\frac{3}{8}'' \times 8\frac{3}{4}''$.
Peoples, Popular, Reform or Mikado: $15''' - 2\frac{3}{4}'' \times 8''$, $20''' - 4'' \times 8''$.
Peoples or Popular: $10''' - 2\frac{3}{16}'' \times 7\frac{3}{4}''$.
Lucisca: $3\frac{7}{16}'' \times 7\frac{7}{8}''$.
Odin: $16''' - 2\frac{11}{16}'' \times 8\frac{1}{2}''$, $20''' - 3\frac{7}{16}'' \times 8\frac{1}{4}''$.
Wizard: $10''' - 2\frac{3}{16}'' \times 7\frac{3}{4}''$, $15''' - 2\frac{11}{16}'' \times 8\frac{1}{2}''$, $16''' - 3\frac{1}{4}'' \times 8\frac{1}{4}''$, $20''' - 4'' \times 8''$.
Britannic, Wanzer, Hitchcock, Kranzow, Pucca: $\frac{7}{8}''$.
Queens Reading Petroleum: $14''' - 1\frac{1}{4}''$.
Silber: $2\frac{3}{4}''$.
Kelly, Luna or Pixie Wick:

000	00	0	1	$1\frac{1}{2}$	2	$2\frac{1}{2}$	3
$\frac{1}{16}''$	$\frac{5}{64}''$	$\frac{3}{32}''$	$\frac{7}{64}''$	$\frac{1}{8}''$	$\frac{9}{64}''$	$\frac{5}{32}''$	$\frac{11}{64}''$

Torch or Duck Wick (Davy): $\frac{3}{16}''$, $\frac{1}{4}''$, $\frac{5}{16}''$, $\frac{3}{8}''$, $\frac{7}{16}''$, $\frac{1}{2}''$, $\frac{5}{8}''$, $\frac{3}{4}''$, $1''$, $1\frac{1}{8}''$.

Wicks for lamps burning colza oil
Flat Colza Tape: $\frac{1}{2}''$, $\frac{5}{8}''$, $\frac{3}{4}''$, $\frac{7}{8}''$, $1''$, $1\frac{1}{4}''$, $1\frac{1}{2}''$.
Hollow Colza Tape, Double: $\frac{3}{8}''$, $\frac{1}{2}''$, $\frac{5}{8}''$, $\frac{3}{4}''$, $\frac{7}{8}''$, $1''$, $1\frac{1}{4}''$, $1\frac{1}{2}''$.
Cycle and Van lamp: $\frac{3}{8}''$, $\frac{1}{2}''$, $\frac{5}{8}''$, $\frac{3}{4}''$, $\frac{7}{8}''$, $1''$.
Queen's Reading: $12'''$ $(1\frac{1}{8}'')$, $14''''$ $(1\frac{1}{4}'')$.

Wicks for lamps burning benzolene (also spirit): $\frac{1}{8}''$, $\frac{5}{32}''$, $\frac{3}{16}''$, $\frac{1}{4}''$, $\frac{9}{32}''$, $\frac{5}{16}''$, $\frac{3}{8}''$, $\frac{7}{16}''$, $\frac{1}{2}''$, $\frac{9}{16}''$, $\frac{5}{8}''$, $\frac{3}{4}''$, $\frac{7}{8}''$, $1''$.

Dimensions of Principal Central Draught Wicks

(Measured flat when folded. Circular unless otherwise stated.)
Ariel: $16''' - 1\frac{11}{16}'' \times 8\frac{1}{2}''$, $20''' - 1\frac{7}{8}'' \times 8\frac{1}{2}''$, $30''' - 2\frac{5}{8}'' \times 9''$.
Court: $16''' - 1\frac{1}{2}'' \times 8''$, $20''' - 2'' \times 8\frac{1}{2}''$, $30''' - 2'' \times 8\frac{1}{2}''$.
Delite: $2'' \times 8\frac{1}{2}''$.
Defries: $10''' - 1\frac{13}{16}'' \times 5''$, $20''' - 1\frac{15}{16}'' \times 6\frac{1}{2}''$, $15''' - 1'' \times 6\frac{1}{2}''$; No. $1 - 1\frac{5}{8}'' \times 7\frac{7}{8}''$, No. $2 - 2'' \times 7\frac{5}{8}''$, No. $3 - 2\frac{5}{8}'' \times 8\frac{5}{8}''$.
English Sun or Marvel: $15''' - 1\frac{5}{8}'' \times 7\frac{3}{4}''$, $20''' - 2'' \times 7\frac{3}{4}''$, $30''' - 2\frac{5}{8}'' \times 10''$.
Famos: 1924 model flat— 90 c.p., $2\frac{7}{8}'' \times 8''$; 1925 model circular— 90 c.p., $1\frac{3}{8}'' \times 10''$.
Helios: see Ariel.
Hinks: $20''' - 45$ c.p.; $2'' \times 7\frac{1}{2}''$; $30''' - 80$ c.p., $2\frac{5}{8}'' \times 10''$.
Invicta: see Venus.
Juno: $14''' - 20$ c.p., $1\frac{1}{2}'' \times 8''$; $20''' - 50$ c.p., $2'' \times 8\frac{1}{2}''$; $30''' - 100$ c.p., $2\frac{5}{8}'' \times 8\frac{3}{4}''$; $60''' - 200$ c.p., $4\frac{1}{4}'' \times 8''$.
Litenite: see Sunlight.
Lampe Belge: see Juno (English).
Morelite: see Sunlight.
Miller: Jnr., $1\frac{1}{4}'' \times 6\frac{3}{8}''$; No. 1, $1\frac{13}{16}'' \times 7\frac{3}{8}''$; No. 2, $2\frac{1}{2}'' \times 7\frac{1}{2}''$; No. 3, $4\frac{1}{4}'' \times 8''$.
Nusunlite: $1\frac{5}{8}'' \times 7\frac{3}{4}''$.
Orion, Superba, Britelite: $14''' - 1\frac{7}{16}'' \times 6\frac{3}{4}''$.

Rochester: Jnr., $1\frac{1}{4}''$ x $5''$; No. 1, $1\frac{13}{16}''$ x $6\frac{3}{4}''$; No. 2, $2\frac{1}{2}''$ x $7''$; No. 3 or 10, $4\frac{1}{4}''$ x $8''$.
Sunlight: $1\frac{3}{4}''$ x $9''$.
Rarelite: $1\frac{13}{16}''$ x $8\frac{3}{4}''$.
Thermidor: No. 1, $1\frac{13}{16}''$ x $5\frac{1}{4}''$.
Trilux: $20'''$—$2''$ x $8\frac{1}{2}''$; $30'''$—$2\frac{5}{8}''$ x $8\frac{3}{4}''$.
Venus or Viking: $14'''$—$1\frac{1}{2}''$ x $8''$; $20'''$—$1\frac{7}{8}''$ x $8\frac{1}{2}''$; $30'''$— $2\frac{5}{8}''$ x $9''$.
Veritas: $20'''$—$1\frac{15}{16}''$ x $8\frac{3}{4}''$; $30'''$—$2\frac{5}{8}''$ x $9\frac{5}{8}''$; $60'''$—$4\frac{3}{8}''$ x $10''$.
Vulcan: $14'''$—$1\frac{5}{16}''$ x $10\frac{1}{4}''$; $16'''$—$1\frac{3}{4}''$ x $10\frac{1}{4}''$; $18'''$—$1\frac{7}{8}''$ x $10\frac{1}{4}''$; $24'''$—$2\frac{1}{4}''$ x $10\frac{3}{4}''$; $30'''$—$2\frac{3}{4}''$ x $12''$.
Union (W. & B.): No. 0, $1\frac{1}{4}''$ x $8''$; No. 1, $1\frac{3}{4}''$ x $10''$; No. 2, $2\frac{3}{8}''$ x $11''$; No. 10, $4\frac{1}{4}''$ x $11\frac{3}{4}''$.
Wonder: $10'''$—$1\frac{5}{16}''$ x $5\frac{1}{4}''$.
Blitz: $20'''$—$2\frac{1}{16}''$ x $7\frac{1}{2}''$; $30'''$—$2\frac{5}{8}''$ x $8\frac{1}{2}''$.
International and Teroso:
National, Royal, Southwark: as Juno.
Daylight and Annular: as English Sun.
Minerva: as English Sun.
Torrex, Arro, Esso: $2\frac{11}{16}''$ x $9''$.

Central Draught Wicks

Principal lamps listed by diameter of wick measured *flat*.

$\frac{13}{16}''$	Defries $10'''$, Thermidor
$1''$	Defries $15'''$
$1\frac{1}{4}''$	Miller Junior, Rochester Junior, Union 0
$1\frac{5}{16}''$	Defries $20'''$, Wonder $10'''$, Vulcan $14'''$
$1\frac{3}{8}''$	Famos 90 1925
$1\frac{1}{2}''$	Court $16'''$, Juno $14'''$, Venus $14'''$, Viking $14'''$, Invicta $14'''$
$1\frac{5}{8}''$	Defries 1, English Sun $15'''$, Nusunlite, Raylite, Marvel $15'''$
$1\frac{11}{16}''$	Ariel $16'''$, Helios $16'''$
$1\frac{3}{4}''$	Sunlight, Union 1, Vulcan $16'''$
$1\frac{13}{16}''$	Miller 1, Rochester 1, Rarelite, Carmen
$1\frac{7}{8}''$	Ariel $20'''$, Helios $20'''$, Venus $20'''$, Viking $20'''$, Invicta $20'''$, Vulcan $18'''$ $20'''$, Vulcan $18'''$
$1\frac{15}{16}''$	Veritas $20'''$
$2''$	Court $20'''$, Delite, Defries 2, English Sun $20'''$, Juno $20'''$, Trilux $20'''$, Marvel $20'''$
$2\frac{1}{16}''$	Blitz $20'''$
$2\frac{1}{4}''$	Vulcan $24'''$
$2\frac{3}{8}''$	Union 2
$2\frac{1}{2}''$	Miller 2, Rochester 2
$2\frac{5}{8}''$	Ariel $30'''$, Court $30'''$, Defries 3, English Sun $30'''$, Helios $30'''$, Juno $30'''$, Veritas $30'''$, Venus $30'''$, Viking $30'''$, Invicta $30'''$, Trilux $30'''$, Blitz $30'''$, Marvel $30'''$
$2\frac{3}{4}''$	Vulcan $30'''$

INDEX

Printed by C. I. Thomas & Sons (Haverfordwest) Ltd.
Merlin's Bridge, Haverfordwest, Pembrokeshire.